Living Reality

A Collection Of Inspirational Poems

by

Audrey M. Virges

TRUTH BOOK PUBLISHERS

First Printing 2009

Printed in the United States of America

ISBN 978-1-935298-21-2   1-935298-21-6

1. Poetry 2. Inspirational 3. Religion

Truth Book Publishers
824 Bills Rd.
Franklin, IL 62638
www.truthbookpublishers.com
877-649-9092

REVIEWS

My wife poems are inspirational because that which comes from the heart reaches the heart. Being inspired by God, she writes about everyday life, the poems lifts you up and make you want to run on and see what the end is going to be. Keep writing baby and one day you'll hear God say "WELL DONE"

LOVE YOUR HUSBAND, SAMUEL VIRGES

These poems were written with an open mind to allow God in, a discipline mind to obey God, and wisdom and understanding to know each of us were born to complete a certain purpose. These poems are inspirational, spiritual, and family oriented. God has given you a great gift and provided you with a blessing to share with others.

YOUR SISTER, DENISE ROBINSON COLLINS

Mrs. Virges poetry will often guide you to a place of quiet rest. It is comforting and lovingly written to encourage you with the assurance that you are still in God's care. Her poems will give you confidence for strength that you are hurting for. Reading her work, you can encounter timeless scriptural wisdom and it will deepen your hunger for more of the same.

PASTOR TYRONE ORR, NEW PROSPECT MISSIONARY BAPTIST CHURCH

Audrey's poems are words from her heart. She truly trusts God to guide her and direct her path; her poems inspire a reader's heart, and that which comes from the heart reaches the heart.

REV. ALTON VIRGES

Your poems inspire me most because they're not just words. They speak life and are designed to do just what the word say do: exhort, rebuke, lift up, and straighten out. I am truly blessed and inspired by them.

REV. GREGORY CLARK

Your poems and quotes are very inspiring not only to the heart, but are uplifting to the soul. May God bless you sis. Virges

REV. LEE BRUNER

ACKNOWLEDGEMENTS

I thank God for this gift of writing inspirational poetry.
Thanks to my family for their love and support. Thanks to
those who have been an inspiration to me. Thanks to my
church family and friends for their encouragements.

Living Reality

A Collection Of Inspirational Poems

by

Audrey M. Virges

TABLE OF CONTENTS

PREFACE

In May 2007, I received a divine gift of writing inspirational poetry, which I am very thankful for. My poems simply imply that with God's help we can make it through the struggles of everyday life. No matter what we go through, He is the answer. I hope you enjoy this book that it may be an inspiration to you.

Audrey M. Virges

LET GOD HANDLE IT

There are problems in life

That we can't handle

Sometimes we think we can.

God can solve any problems that we have

He made us He's the man.

If we attempt to solve our problems

Then God will leave them alone.

The way we go about solving them

Twice as much will surely go wrong.

Sometimes it's best to keep silent

As a baby bird in a nest

Don't let your temper get the best of you

Or you'll really make a mess.

Let God handle it because He can

He can see way farther than we can see.

The results may not come out the way we think

But it'll come out the way it's supposed to be.

Audrey M. Virges

GOD IS OUR REFUGE AND STRENGH, A VERY
PRESENT HELP IN TROUBLE.

PSALM 46.1

IT'S BETTER TO GIVE THAN TO RECEIVE

It's better to give than to receive,

Because you are truly able.

If you are on the receiving end

You have nothing to put on the table.

It's better to give than to receive.

All's well with your home so fine,

But there's someone homeless to help standing in the soup line.

It's better to give than to receive.

Just because you're fareing well today?

You could very well be on the receiving end,

Just two or three days away.

It's better to give than to receive.

God want us to lend a helping hand,

When someone's in need.

We should do all we can.

It's better to give than to receive.

It's a blessing to be able to do,

Give all you can that it may be a blessing.

The receiver may one day be you.

Audrey M. Virges

Give, and it shall be given unto you; good measure, pressed down, and shaken together, and running over, shall men give into your bosom. For with the same measure that ye mete withal it shall be measured to you again.

LUKE 6.38

ALWAYS PRAY

When God woke you this morning, were you thankful enough to pray?

Did you thank him for awakening you, allowing you to see a brand new day?

Did you thank him for your family, other church families as well as the one you belong?

Did you thank him for your enemies, for even they can make you strong?

Did you thank God for Jesus, who hung, bled, and died on Calvary?

And are you most thankful that He rose, with all power in his hands you see?

We should be prayerful at all times, not just when we're going through.

Pray during the good times and the bad, that's the way God's children do.

Prayer will fix it every time; pray to God, He stays on the mainline.

He may not come when you want him, but I guarantee He'll come on time.

Pray without ceasing, that's what 1st Thess: 5.17 say do.

If Jesus had to pray, what do you think about me and you?

So keep praying, morning, noon, and night,

The battle is not yours; the battle is the Lord's to fight.

Pray without ceasing, each and every day

For the bible say man should always pray.

Audrey M. Virges

PRAY WITHOUT CEASING

I THESSALONIANS 5.17

NEVER GIVE UP ON YOUR DREAM

Never give up on your dream.

It may not be as hard to achieve,

As you make it seem.

But you do know there's work that has to be done,

So start striving and try to make it fun.

In the midst of your toiling,

Say I can, I can, and I can.

Because achieving your dreams to you is a great demand.

Work hard and be steadfast,

Not a moment to delay.

Never give up on your dreams,

And you'll achieve your dream one day.

Audrey M. Virges

WEEPING MAY ENDURE FOR A NIGHT
BUT JOY COMETH IN THE MORNING

Weeping may endure for a night,

But joy cometh in the morning.

But will in the morning be tomorrow,

Or another day of weeping to endure?

If in the morning was tomorrow

All night would we stay awake

Anticipating the joy that would await at daybreak.

When trouble comes it seem to hang in there a long time

But there's hope in Jesus, He'll give ease to a trouble mind.

So many times in the morning is not tomorrow,

But God will ease the pain until the morning come.

Keep praying and hang on in there

God's will   must be done.

If in the morning is not tomorrow

Keep trusting God for a new day of adorning,

Because weeping may endure for a night

But joy cometh in the morning.

Audrey M. Virges

WEEPING MAY ENDURE FOR A NIGHT, BUT JOY
COMETH IN THE MORNING

PSALM 30.5b

IF WE HELP SOMEONE ALONG LIFE'S JOURNEY, THEN OUR LIVING WILL NOT BE IN VAIN.

If we help someone along life's journey, then our living will
not be in vain.

Three generations will have passed away

And no one will remember you.

But in God's mind the wonderful things you did will always
remain.

The things you do to make your living not be in vain

You'll surely do them from your heart

Because people can feel whether they are real or not,

And if it's not don't even attempt to start.

If you help someone along this life's journey

God will strengthen you with what you have to do.

For that same manner of help in which you gave

Will one day come back to you.

The more we pray more helpful we become

More strength in God we'll gain

If we help someone along this life's journey

Our living will not be in vain.

Audrey M. Virges

THERE'S A BLESSING IN EVERY BURDEN

There's a blessing in every burden

Even though the burden is hard to bear.

But God will help you bear it

He will bring you up for air.

There's a blessing in every burden

You can't really see it at the time.

Burdens can get heavy

They'll make you whimper and whine.

There's a blessing in every burden

To one that's weak or to one that's strong.

The burden that seems the worst

Are the burdens of being done wrong.

From a burden a blessing will come

Right then what it will be we don't know.

For that huge water wave out in the sea

Trickled down as it came to shore.

For every burden there is a purpose

From every blessing happiness flow.

There will not be a burden yet

That God can't help you through.

So thank him for your burdens

They you won't forget.

There's a blessing in every burden

That God will give you yet.

O give thanks unto the LORD; for he is good: for his mercy endureth for ever.

Psalms 118.29

DON'T LET YOUR LIFE GET DERAILED

Don't let your life get derailed thinking   that you know and don't.

Pray to God for wisdom,

He'll give it to you, don't think he want.

Life is uncertain,

It has its ups and downs.

As we pursue its challenges,

We'll make it round by round.

Don't let your life get derailed putting your trust in man.

Put your trust in God,

He'll always hold your hand.

And just in case your life got derailed and everything got outta whack,

Turn it over to God.

He'll put you back on track.

GOD GAVE US FRIENDS

(YOU ARE MY FRIEND)

You are my friend

Because you care what I feel.

You are my friend

Because you don't pretend you're for real.

You are my friend

Because you want what's best for me,

You are my friend

Because we pray together you see.

You are my friend

Because your compassionate benevolent words help me
through hard times.

You are my friend

Even if you don't have a dime.

You are my friend

No matter where you work.

You are my friend

Whether a lawyer, factory worker or candy store clerk.

Audrey M. Virges

You see God gave us friends

They help us in need

You are my friend

My friend in deed.

In order to gain friends, show yourself friendly.

DON'T WORRY

Don't worry when your job lay off

God knows your body needs rest.

Don't worry when a lot of things go wrong

You're only being put to a test.

Don't worry when your vehicle breaks down

And you have to park it in the shade.

If they never did break down

People would be driving the first ones ever made.

Don't worry if you become ill

And there's nothing you can do.

Pray to God for healing

And trust he'll bring you through.

If you worry your hair will fall out

You'll be half bald that you can believe.

Then you'll have to spend money

Going to buy some weave.

You see problems come as long as we live

If you worry you'll make one problem be two.

Turn that one problem over to Jesus

That's the best you can ever do.

Don't Worry Be Happy

WORK WITHIN YOUR CALLING

God gave you all a gift or calling.

Because He knows what's best for you.

If you work within your calling,

You'll be the best at what you do.

If you work within your calling

You shouldn't strain your mind to hard

Because the work you've been called to do?

Always in your life will it be a part.

If you work within your calling

People will commend you and say go ahead,

Because they see that what you do

Is nothing that you dread?

Because God gave you a calling,

And it consists of the things you do.

Work within your calling

Because it makes you be you.

Audrey M. Virges

And there are differences of administrations, but the same
Lord

I CORINTHIANS 12.5

PRIDE

Pride is something we should not have

Not even one day out of the week.

It causes us to be puffed up,

And humbleness we will not seek.

Pride will make you seek to be a leader

When your character say's you're a follower.

Pride will let you go hungry

Because you refuse to ask for a dollar.

Pride will make you pretend you know

When you really have no concern.

Before you're confronted with the situation again,

You have to hurry seek and learn.

Pride will make you spend money

Trying to keep up with someone else,

You don't know how they got what they have

Might put a strain on your health.

So put pride aside

And be humble in every way.

Put pride aside

And be humble every day.

Audrey M. Virges

When pride cometh, then cometh shame: but with the lowly
is wisdom.

Proverbs 11.2

THERE ARE PEOPLE IN THIS WORLD

There are people in this world
Who are struggling every day. Some are on drugs and alcohol
Thinking it will help them find their way.
There are people in this world, who only need a smile
That it may lift their spirit, and help them go the extra mile.
There are people in this world, who are in the nursing home?
If only their relatives would visit them, they wouldn't feel abandoned and alone.
There are people in this world, who only need a word
From some friend that they trust, and can be confronted from what they heard.
There are people in this world, whose child have been killed in the street.
Now they lay awake at night, can't sleep, no appetite to eat.
There are people in this world, starving moms, dads, sisters, and brothers.
Too big in one place, not big enough in another.
There are people in this world, who say it's hard to live on
Because their relatives have already been called home.
There are people in this world, whose marriage was so sweet
Yet it ended up in divorce and defeat.
But there's a solution, He's invisible to you and I,
We can feel his power so strong.
God made the world and you and I in it
He's there when everything goes wrong.

Audrey M. Virges

He say call him up I'm right here
It won't cost you a dime.
Call him anytime; He stays on the main line.
Call him up He's always awake
Put your trust in him He'll never leave you
Nor will you He forsake.

SUNDAY MORNING WORSHIP

Sunday morning worship is as uplifting as can be.
We are very excited to get there
To get our souls revived you see.
Sunday school was taught wonderfully
Most commented on the lesson well
It takes a lot of teaching now days
And quite a bit of bible drill.
Time now for worship service to began
O' what great singing when the praise team sings
Everyone singing along saying amen
Lifting Jesus name and clapping their hand.
After benevolent offering, alter call, and collection
The choir is ready to do their thing.
They sing the most uplifting songs there are
And to God great praises they bring.
Now it's time for the pastor to preach
For he has been preparing his sermon throughout the week.
He preaches hard trying to pull someone out of the pit.
At the end of the sermon some come some sit.
Sunday morning worship as uplifting as can be.
Come next Sunday, another great service of worship you'll
see.

Audrey M. Virges

Not forsaking the assembling of ourselves together, as the manner of some is; but exhorting one another: and so much the more, as ye see the day approaching.
HEBREWS 10.25

PRAY AND BELIEVE AND YOU'LL RECEIVE
PRAY AND DOUBT AND YOU'LL DO WITHOUT.

Powerful things happen when you pray and believe.
Whatever is in God's will for you,
Believe and you'll receive.
But as sure as you pray
And you're already in doubt
Everything you prayed for
You'll surely do without.
Pray and believe and you'll receive
Whether it's something big or small.
God has cattle on a thousand hills
He's able to give it to you all.
So trust in him with all your heart
Then doubt will not within you be a part.
So as sure as you pray and believe
Get ready for your blessing
That you're going to receive.

But without faith it is impossible to please him: for he that
cometh to God must believe that he is, and that he is a
rewarder of them that diligently seek him.
HEBREWS 11.6

JESUS IS EVERYTHING TO ME

Jesus is my all and all
He is everything to me
He loved us so much He suffered for us
He died on Calvary.

Jesus is everything to me
My shelter from the storm.
He's the cool breeze in the summer
He's the heat in the winter to keep me warm.

Jesus is everything to me
He's my strength when I'm weak.
I pray to him daily
To keep me strong, humble, and meek.

Jesus is everything to me
My protector in every way
He hides me in the shadow of his wings,
And keep me safe day by day.

Jesus is everything to me
He's family in a distant land.
He'll be a friend when friends are few
He's always there to hold my hand.

Jesus is ever thing to me
He's every breath I take
He guides me through the day
He balances every step I make.

I could go on and on and on
About his omnipotent awesome power you see.
I don't know what He is to you
I know he's everything to me.

If it hadn't been for the Lord on my side.

THE OLD HOME PLACE FARM

On the old home place farm great sentiment lie.
I cherished wonderful memories there I can't deny
The early morning biscuits were very big and fluffy.
The butter grandma churned was yellow and puffy.
The water pumped from the well was very cool and clear
Down at the barn the smell of cows and hay filled the air.
The fruit trees were ripe, and fruit fell to the ground.
There were also moles under the yard's surface and that
really made us frown.
The acres of land were many so the field was a good walk
away.
That's where grandma and grandpa made their living each
and every day.
These were the good old days
How great was the charm
I wouldn't trade anything for the memory of that
Old home place farm.

WE ARE VERY BLESSED

Whether you believe it or not
We are very blessed.
Because God woke us this morning
And with Jesus in our lives
That's blessed at its best.
So what if we don't drive the finest car,
Or eat in the finest restaurants every meal
Or have money to throw away
Like as do some of the big wheels.
What if the clothes we wear
Are not really the top of the line?
We are still truly blessed,
Just keep them neatly ironed.
What if the home in which we live
Is not a mansion on the hill?
We are truly blessed with what we have
That we can afford to pay the bills.
And your job you have your blessed with
Although you have no degree?
Do it to the best of your ability
For it will help you meet your needs
If you think you're not blessed
Take a deep breath
And see if the air is yours to give.
If you think you're not blessed
Began losing your breath,
Then will no other blessing matter but to live.

IT'S YOUR BIRTHDAY

Yes it's your birthday
A wonderful day to be adorned.
God knew your name before conception,
And He had a special day for you to be born.

O the joy you have brought
Since you have entered this world.
Brought endless joy to your family,
Being more precious than a pearl.

You bring so much joy
To your many friends
Sometimes we wonder
When it all begin

So make the most of this birthday
God's blessing he bestow.
Hold tightly to his hand
Pray He let you see many more.

Audrey M. Virges

NOT THIS TIME

Not this time will the same thing be done.

Because God has given me a different view.

Not this time will I live the same old way,

Because God have made my life brand new.

Not this time will I think I know and don't,

Because wisdom God has given me.

Not this time will I doubt what I can do?

With God the best is yet to be.

Not this time will I go without

When all I have to do is ask,

God will supply my every need,

And help me with any task.

I'll put my trust in him,

I know He won't leave me behind.

I can't afford not to trust him

O no! Not this time.

Wisdom resteth in the heart of him that hath understanding

Proverbs 14.33a

WHEN LIFE WAS SIMPLE

When life was simple

We were small

Playing in the dirt

Without a care at all

When life was simple

We climbed trees.

The only worry we had

Was skinning our knees.

When life was simple

We had no bills to pay.

Not knowing that in years to come

We had to find our own way.

That day came a bit too fast

No more playing in the dirt

No more going to class.

Now we're experiencing every day

Having to get up with bills to pay.

Facing problems from simply not knowing.

Had we known we wouldn't have trod that way.

Audrey M. Virges

But life's beautiful. Hang on in there,

And don't you break just bend

For it's a joy to let your mind think back

To when life was simple then.

WHEN THE BEST WE DO IS NOT GOOD ENOUGH

When the best we do is not good enough

What do we do then?

Do we keep striving to make our best better,

Or do we throw in the towel

And hold our chin?

When the best we do is not good enough

We lose our sense of inspiration.

Go to God in prayer

He's got the combination.

When the best we do is not good enough

We cannot stop in our tracks.

Pray to God for motivation

He'll help us make a comeback.

When the best we do is not good enough

Keep pressing forward is what to do

Don't give up, continue to strive

Depend on God to help us through.

Keep striving

BE YOURSELF AND YOU WON'T HAVE TO CHANGE

God gave all of us a personality

And ourselves He expects us to be.

Don't act a different way, or act like someone else

That's only fake or pretence you see.

If you say one thing over here,

Over there also say the same.

Just be yourself, and you won't have to change.

If you know you're a noisy person,

Don't pretend around some people that you're quiet.

Just be yourself, and you 'll have nothing to hide.

Just as sure as you act different

Than the way you supposed to be,

The truth will come out,

Then you'll be embarrassed you see.

God gave you a personality

It, don't try to rearrange.

Just be yourself

And you won't have to change.

OUR YARD IS BEAUTIFUL

OUR yard is beautiful

As a picture on a shelf.

We work in it diligently

Landscaped it myself.

We have thirty-four hedges shaped like a t,

I keep them trimmed and mulched so neat.

We have two sets of cannons

On each side of the yard.

They multiply so quickly

They grow together both parts.

My husband mows the lawn

How beautiful is the grass

It's amazing whether it rain or not

Only a week will it last.

We love our yard

And admire its beauty each day,

But we have to keep it up

For it to remain that way.

Hard work is not in vain.

WAIT ON THE LORD

If there are things in your life

That you want to acquire or achieve

And you think you're not getting them fast enough?

Do yourself a favor and wait on the lord

If you don't you'll make your own life tough

If you wait on the lord blessing will come

In a way that's most divine, you know how we'll buy things

And don't consult the lord first, and a bill might fall behind?

There's a purpose in life in everything we go through

Even orphans in an orphan home.

If they only wait on the lord

One day the name orphan will be changed into now I'm grown.

Waiting on the lord requires weathering many storms

So when we take them to the alter leave them there.

Make sure you don't take them back home

If you do they'll be harder to bear.

Let patience have its perfect work

In our lives, and just you believe

That we have to have reached a level of spiritual maturity

Before a lot of blessing we can receive.

They that wait upon the lord, blessing will come so great

Just wait on the lord

On the lord just you wait.

Wait on the LORD: be of good courage, and he shall
strengthen thine heart: wait, I say, on the LORD.

Psalms 27.14

EXERCISE

We should have a good habit of exercise

Because it helps our body be healthy.

It needs to be a part of our daily life

Whether poor, or whether wealthy.

So start walking a little every day

At first take your time

Then practice more and more,

You'll really get unwinded.

Exercise seems a bit easier

When we lay off those stewed tomatoes.

It gets easier than that

When we push away those mashed potatoes.

It's all good when you can eat with moderation,

Exercising have your way.

It's nothing wrong with exercising three times a week

But it's best to do it every day.

IF YOU COULD LIVE YOUR LIFE OVER

If you could live your life over, what choices would you make?

Would you make the same choices or another avenue would you take.

If you could live your life over, would you help your fellowman?

Would you show love, would you share?

Or would you close your hand up and be self centered,

And not at all would you care?

If is only two letters, and it means on the condition that,

But then if all if's and but's were candy and nuts

We would have a merry Christmas and that's a fact.

Some people say o if i could just turn back the hands of time

How different it would be, but you can't turn it back,

Trust Jesus the rest of the way, faith goes where the eyes can't see.

If you could live your life over

Would you remember thy creator in the days of thy youth?

Or would you be ungrateful and illogical, and lie rather than tell the truth.

If you could live your life over

Would you ask God to help you, or would you continue
thinking you could make it your own?

Because the weight of decision making fall on you by the
time you get grown.

With Jesus you don't have to wish to turn back the hand of
time.

He'll help you go forward and value life so divine.

We can plan our life so well, just like we dreamed it to be

But if everything went the way we planned

We wouldn't feel the need for prayer you see.

So start now and go forward

Not a moment to delay

Ask God to guide you

The rest of the way.

Wait on the LORD: be of good courage, and he shall
strengthen thine heart: wait, I say, on the LORD.

Ecclesiastes 12.1a

MOM YOU ARE MORE PRECIOUS THAN ANY JEWEL TO ME

Mom you're more precious

Than any jewel to me.

More precious than rubies

More precious than sapphires

More precious than diamonds you see.

You bore me into this world

Yet you are my gift.

Every time I wanted to be held

You gave me that pleasurable lift.

As I grew you nurtured me,

And taught me right from wrong.

Cause you wanted me to live my best for God,

And have a happy life and home.

Just as I know you cherished my love

I cherish your love also.

You have supported me in every way

More than any diamond can glow.

You're more precious than any jewel to me.

No matter how they shine.

Mom you are a gift to me.

Because God made you mine.

Wait on the LORD: be of good courage, and he shall
strengthen thine heart: wait, I say, on the LORD

Proverbs 31.15ab

DAD YOU'RE THE MAN

Dad you are my hero

You really are the man.

I thank God for giving you to me

I love the way you take a stand.

Dad you are my hero

You taught me so many things.

You rewarded me for doing good,

And you disciplined me when I did wrong.

Dad you are my hero

For our family you did your best

You provided for us a good living

And helped us to pass every test.

Dad you are my hero

You taught me to take a stand.

Dad you are my hero

Dad you're the man

Hear, ye children, the instruction of a father, and attend to
know understanding.

Proverbs 4.1

MAKE THE MOST OF EVERY DAY

Each day we awake is another blessing.

Thank God for waking us from our nightly resting.

Now we're wondering what this day will bring,

Actually hoping for sunshine instead of rain.

Now we're up and all afresh

God's goodness that He bestow

This a day to live our fullest,

Because we've never seen this day before.

We go to work every day

No mistakes can we afford.

It's such a blessing to be able to work,

We should do our work as unto the Lord

We should make the most of every day

Its wonders to discover.

Live each day as if it was our last,

And pray God let us see another.

WE ARE BLESSED TO BE A BLESSING

God bless us to bless others

In a very giving way.

Whether a word of kindness or financial blessing

Or a love package per say.

Bless people with your time

Speak blessings upon them on the phone.

Bless someone with your visit

To them in the nursing home.

Our blessing is not in what we have

But what we have to give

To help someone less fortunate than we

To show love because we live.

So to someone be a blessing

It'll come back just you see.

God showed us how to give

Giving is the key.

HAVE YOU THOUGHT ABOUT

Have you thought about how paper is made

From trees how they stand so tall?

That it's used in every school

In every room from hall to hall?

Have you thought about the water

How it look so blue in the sea?

But if you dipped some up in a glass

It would be a different color to you and me.

Have you thought about the stars

How beautiful they are at night?

Yet in the morning, they'll still there

Only dispelled by the light.

Have you ever thought about the horizon

How it look as though it would end?

Yet if we drove five hundred miles

Over there it would look the same way again.

Have you thought about the ditch

On the side of the road so dry.

When it rain and over flow

You can catch fish there just as sure as you try.

When we think of a lot of things

Some we don't understand them to be.

God created everything for a purpose

That's the way He made it to be.

NO ONES EXEMPT

No one's exempt from the trials of this life

Yet laughter will always be.

For it takes both actions to make this body live

One mind carries them both you see.

No one's exempt from being talked about

Whether they do bad or good.

Some will say you didn't do good enough,

Some will say you did the best you could

No one's exempt for illness

Even though it's just a cold

Illness will come as sure as you live

From the least young to the very old

No one is exempt from death

From the nearest resident to farthest mile

But you can laugh at things a love one did

And make the thought worthwhile.

No one's exempt when preached to

Of the things we fail to do,

So when the preacher steps on our toes, shape up

And better should we strive to do.

For it is written, As I live, saith the Lord, every knee shall bow to me, and every tongue shall confess to God.

Romans 14.11

OUR CHILDREN IN SCHOOL

Our children in school have come a very long way.

My husband and I can remember their very first day.

As we took them to kindergarten class

While holding their little hand,

They being too young to comprehend

That education would be a demand.

They met new friends, and

Learned of airplanes, and motorcycles.

Our son Craig at six years old? Change his name to Michael.

Our daughter Samantha changed her hairstyle

After she got on the bus,

Our baby boy Jeremy didn't play, neither did he care to fuss.

When they knew they had to cram and study for a test?

All they wanted to do was eat, play, and rest.

When they carelessly failed a test

And volunteered to wash the dishes

That trick didn't work with Sam and I

We still spank those britches.

School years passed very fast, now they'll all become grown.

Experiencing life now with children of their own.

They with their children in school again.

Now we're grandparents

Lending a loving helping hand.

Lo, children are an heritage of the LORD: and the fruit of the womb is his reward.

Psalms 127.3

ANGER

Anger tampers with your mind

In a way that's really unreal,

It will make you say things that you regret you said

And do what you shouldn't do and feel what you should not feel.

When you feel yourself getting angry

It's best to stop and pray.

For God to guide you around your anger.

You know he will, He's the way.

Anger will break up relationships,

Some people never speak again.

It has no respect of persons

It will damage a girl, boy, woman, or man.

Anger will make you sick

If it you can't control,

It will elevate your blood pressure

And on your body it can take a toll.

So in an unpleasant situation

Stop and think what's best for you.

Pray to God for comfort

Your mind he will renew.

A soft answer turneth away wrath: but grievous words
stir up anger.

Proverbs 15.1

GOD MADE US, HE KNOWS HOW WE FEEL.

AND HE CAN FIX US.

God made us and knows every intention of our heart

He knows us from our head to our toe.

There's nothing that can go wrong with us that He can't fix

There's nothing that he didn't know.

There's nothing that you can go through,

That He don't know how you feel

There's not a problem that he can't fix, or a sickness He can't heal.

When family and friends treat you like they don't know?

Jesus said give it to me I know how it feel.

Because peter denied me three times

Before time for the cock to crow.

When you lose a love one the pain is hard and not easy to accept

Trust Jesus to ease the pain when Lazarus died Jesus wept.

Jesus gave sight to the blind, unstopped dear ears, healed a withered hand

That and many more miracles He did just at his command.

When you have a headache, Jesus can heal it,

Because He know how it feel,

Because a crown of thorns was pressed down upon his head

Right there on Calvary's hill

So whatever is the problem, whatever is the deal

Jesus can fix it, He know what you feel.

IN TIMES OF SORROW

In times of sorrow life is hard

I am as sorry as can be.

God's will must be done in our lives

He'll mend the hurt you see.

Be encouraged. No matter who God take from you

Life has to go on.

It's a joy to know that you'll meet them again

In that heavenly home.

So keep smiling and lift Jesus name

And do it o so bold.

He'll always be your comfort

You in his arms he'll hold.

Blessed are they that mourn: for they shall be comforted.

MATTHEW 5.4

LOOK FORWARD TO SOMETHING EVERY DAY

To help live life to its fullest

Look forward to something every day.

Plan something inspiring that will

Rejuvenate your mind in every way.

Look forward to something every day

Even if it's a chore.

It will make your life most gratifying

Being satisfied even more.

Look forward to something every day

That will bring a smile to your face.

Then life will not be boring

It will only help you pick up the pace.

Look forward to something every day

Nothing far away, maybe something quite near.

Maybe nothing to earnings

But only a need to volunteer.

Look forward to something every day

Maybe a phone call that will bring a smile

It's looking forward to something every day

That help make life feel worthwhile.

DON'T COMPLAIN

Don't complain about problems

Because complaining will not help.

Be thankful things are as well as they are

Some things in life you just have to accept.

Some people complain and complain

They feel there's nothing else to do.

If you talk to other people about your problems

You'll find out that they have problems too.

Take your complaints and put them on the table

As well as other peoples complaints all in a stack

Nine out of ten times after the complaints are reviewed

You'll hurry and take yours back.

One day can make a difference in your life

It depends on what change it brings

Hold on and count your blessings,

And try not to complain.

Not that I speak in respect of want: for I have learned, in whatsoever state I am, therewith to be content.

Phil. 4.11

DROPPING A HABIT

It's hard to drop a habit

Because it's a habit one love so much.

There are so many different habits

Some people haven't heard the such.

Some people smoke, some dip, some drink

And it is dangerous to their health.

If they would count up the money they spent

Quite a bit was taken from their wealth.

Some people bite their nails, some chew their tongue,

And some people play with their ears

Some people pick up habits

Simply from their peers.

Whatever is your habit

With your desire and prayer you can stop.

Pray that it diminish every day

And soon that habit you'll drop.

Audrey M. Virges

Just believe that you can do it

HOW TIME BRINGS ABOUT A CHANGE

Time brings about a change of course in the way we grow.

At first we were babies then nothing did we know.

As we grew our bodies became strong

Our teeth were sharp and eyesight was keen.

Then we were able to walk and run,

And on no one did we have to lean.

Soon we're in the prime of our life, our career doing just fine.

Some women shaped like coke bottles, men with muscled think they are fine.

Enjoying your family, going out to eat

What delicious steak and fried chicken,

Living each day to its fullest,

But guess what? Time is still ticking.

Approaching the golden years

Time brought about a change,

And now on someone do you have to lean.

Remember the eyesight you once had? Now it's not keen.

And when your shape you thought you would keep

Your muscle not so firm.

Time brought about a change and made you lose your
charm

For most people dentures have taken their place.

Your steps have gotten shorter, you can hardly pick up the
pace.

It's a blessing to get older, even if depending on our
children for most every thing

For if God don't call us home when we're young

Time will bring about a change.

Living to get old is a blessing.

CHILDREN NOW DAYS HAVE NOTHING MUCH TO DO

Children now days have nothing much to do.

No more old time traditions

To make them strong and true.

No more cutting wood with that old sharpen ax,

Instead they're inside chilling out,

Listening to music at it max.

Hardly any more picking berries in the berry patch.

Instead they're counting their clothes

Making sure each set match.

No more over the oven

Do they have to cook and slave.

Everything's so modernized now.

They just pop it in the microwave.

And in school now they need less tooters,

Because in almost every home

There's a nice upgraded computer.

Times have changed from what it used to be,

And the world's all a new

Children nowadays won't be as tough

As the generation before them,

Because they have nothing much to do.

THERE ARE THORNS ON ROSES TOO

As beautiful as life is

Don't expect every day to be sunshine for you

There are rough roads as well as smooth ones

And there are thorns on roses too.

Be encouraged God is able

Trust He'll carry you through

We have to take the bitter with the sweet

Because there are thorns on roses too.

Keep claiming your blessing already done

Keep praying each day your life renew.

Don't be discouraged when things don't go your way

Because there are thorns on roses too.

Just like life roses are beautiful

Just like thorns obstacles await too.

God is larger than any obstacle we have

He's waiting to handle it for you.

For every obstacle God bring you through pluck off a thorn

So around the stem your hand can close.

God carried you through your obstacles

Now you have only a beautiful rose.

WHEN YOU THINK YOU KNOW AND DON'T

When you think you know and don't

It's almost too late.

If you knew what you didn't know ahead of time

You would have nothing to regret or debate.

When you think you know and don't

Listening to someone that know is hard to do

Because you think you know

there's nothing much that they can tell you.

If we awake and everything we knew

Then nothing would be a surprise.

Life then just might be boring

There would be nothing to compromise.

If we knew what we didn't know

No trials would we face.

Then we would gain no strength

In this Christian race.

When you think you know and don't

And no one can tell you so?

That's what life's all about

We have to learn as we go.

GOD WON'T SEND YOU VOICE MAIL

When we feel the need as we always do to go to God in prayer,

He won't send you voice mail.

He'll talk to you right then and there,

He won't put you on hold.

While so long the music play,

For He know your call is important,

Or you wouldn't have called him today.

He don't have a next available representative to put on the line,

Cause he's God all by himself.

He can talk to me, you, they, and them,

And at the same time talk to everyone else.

And you don't have to leave a call back number,

Because He knows you and He know what it is.

Because out of his nostrils he blew into you the breath of life.

And a living soul he made you to live,

So you make your call,

And don't be afraid that your call won't go through

He knows all about you,

And know you're gonna call

He is only waiting on you.

SOW A GOOD SEED

Sow a good seed

Cause you'll reap what you sow

Don't put too much on credit

Cause you'll have to pay what you owe.

You can plant one grain of corn

Many ears will it bring.

If it's a good seed sown

It'll bring sunshine instead of rain.

If you plant a smile,

A smile you'll reap in return.

If you display an arrogant attitude

Away from you people will adjourn.

Do all you can for someone

Especially when you know it's due.

For that same compassion of love

You'll won't to be returned to you.

You may not ever think of

The people you may come to need

So try hard and do your best

To sew a good seed.

Be not deceived; God is not mocked: for whatsoever a man soweth, that shall he also reap.

Galatians 6.7

TRY IT AGAIN

If you ran in a marathon race

And you came in on tail end

If you want to win first place

Don't give up try it again.

If you went on a diet to lose twenty pounds

And you worked out hard and only lost ten,

Be encouraged and have a strong desire

And just you try it again.

If you failed a test in class

And disappointment really set in,

Grab your books and study twice as hard

And just you try it again.

It's not the end if you failed on the first try

Maybe you needed a helping hand

Don't let the first try discourage you

It's a privilege to try again.

Don't give up.

WE SHALL MEET AGAIN

We shall meet again

In this life our love did grow

When we accepted Jesus as our savior

We knew we would meet again on the other shore.

We all have love ones

Who we hold on our hearts so true

But this world is not our home

We're only passing through.

God gave us life and intended our lives for him we live

To show love and compassion

To be helpful and to give.

Isn't it good to know

God has a home prepared

For all his children to live

With him forever up there.

It's a blessing to have known our loves ones

We cherish their love so grand

One day in that sweet bye and bye

We shall meet again

Audrey M. Virges

LET YOUR LIGHT SHINE

Let your light shine

So the world can see

That you have Jesus in your heart

Despite what your problems may be.

Let your light shine

No matter where you go

Whether a ballgame, beauty shop

Or simply at the grocery store.

Let your light shine

No matter who hard you work or where

Work is what it is

Whether inside or outside in the air

Let your light shine

In church on Sunday morning

For there it usually does

Don't let it stop shining after service is over

Always let it shine to show God's love.

Let your light so shine before men, that they may see your good works, and glorify your Father which is in heaven.

Matt. 5.16

THE GIFT

Christmas is a time for giving

To show our heartfelt love.

But God is the greatest gift giver

He gave his son Jesus from above.

There are people who would love to give a gift

But are not able to do so because of financial reasons.

Those are the people one should give a gift to

To bring them cheer in this holiday season.

Jesus our gift laid in a manger

O' what a lowly birth.

But He had to be born to one day die

For all the sins of all people on earth.

So whether or not you can give a gift

It's really doesn't matter it's ok.

Jesus is the reason for the season

Thank God for him today.

Audrey M. Virges

And she shall bring forth a son, and thou shalt call his name JESUS: for he shall save his people from their sins.

Matt. 1.21

THE BEAUTY OF A FLOWER

O the beauty of a flower

After the bloom has blossomed out.

It gives radiance to the earth

It's beauty does with a doubt.

Without a flower the earth would be plain

In order for it to be nourished

God send down showers of rain.

Be thankful for flowers

The enhancement to the earth they give

Their beauty brings us joy

Each day that we live.

THE WEEKEND

Everyone's ready for the weekend

Around about the day of Wednesday

For they know that at the week end

Another check will they get paid.

On the weekend you dine and relax

And enjoy your family and home.

When Uncle Sam has visited your check?

It sometimes make you feel alone.

Pay your tithes first,

It's what God say to do.

What you thought your check wouldn't buy,

God will give the rest to you

We mow the lawn and do other chores on weekends

Through the week it's not so groovy.

Maybe sometimes after Sunday service

We'll have time to go to the movies.

Make the most of your time w

With your family that you spend.

Before you know it, it's Monday morning,

And your weekend has come to an end.

Audrey M. Virges

IF YOU STRIVE TO LEARN, YOU'LL LEARN TO STRIVE

If you strive to learn

You'll do your very best

You'll be persistent in studying hard

In order to pass with a good grade every test.

When you learn to strive

Striving you will automatically do.

The education you are striving for

Will always be a part of you.

In your striving

Say I can, I can, and I can

Because getting an education

Is a great great demand.

Keep believing, don't give up

Pray and keep your dream alive,

If you strive to learn

You will learn to strive.

MORTUARY SERVICE

Mortuary service is a flourishing business because God call soldiers home every day.

When a family calls the mortuary of a death they grab their gear and head that way.

The next day or so give or take a day arrangements have to be made.

Money have to be paid up front or services might be delayed.

Of course the family's in bereavement for from their love one they had to part.

The funeral directors offer heartfelt sympathy and comfort from their heart.

They prepare the body to the family's satisfaction

So when the family comes to view it they'll have a satisfied reaction.

They pick up the immediate family at the home in a limousine, o what a comfortable ride.

It 's the only occasion most people get to ride in one so they take it all in stride.

People come from near some quite a long way.

It's the only time some come to church at all; maybe they'll get saved that day

The choir sings their songs, the pastor preach the eulogy.

Funeral directors back in charge, now they're off to the cemetery.

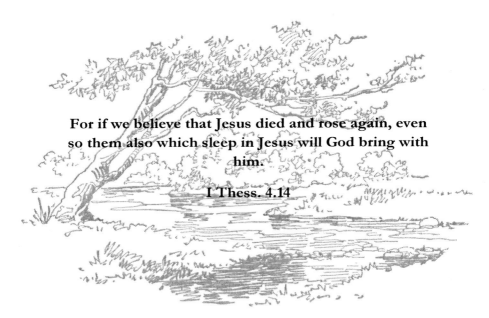

The line long and large, the body is in the ground, the funerals over at last

The family returns to the church for the fellowship and repast.

Funeral directory for this service is almost over now, but not until they take the family home

Which seems a bit easier somehow, even though the funeral's over

The family they don't forget

They keep you in their prayers, and God comfort you yet.

For if we believe that Jesus died and rose again, even so them also which sleep in Jesus will God bring with him.

I Thess. 4.14

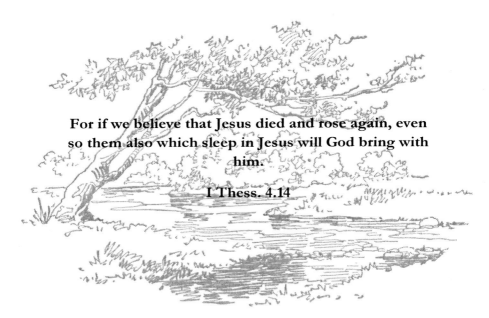

DON'T BE IDOL

Don't be idol

There's work to be done you see.

To make this world a better place

For the comfort of you and me.

Don't be idol be useful

In your community and your home.

Go and visit the elderly

Don't so easily waver or roam.

Give and show compassion to some veteran

That have lost a limb overseas,

Fighting war so far from home

So that our country remains to be free.

Don't be idol be helpful

To a motherless child show love

As sure as you learn to give

God's blessings will overflow from above.

Keeping yourself busy is an asset to you

Continue to do so don't you stop.

Don't let your mind be idol

Cause an idle mind is the devil's workshop.

Audrey M. Virges

IT'S BEST TO WALK AWAY

Someone made you angry

Now you want to fight instead of pray?

You better think about it twice

Most times it's best to walk away

You can take matters in your own hands

Not knowing the consequences you'll have to pay.

Let God fight your battle

Most of the times it's best to walk away.

You may be physically strong

With big muscles and strong thighs

But it's best to walk away

Because bullets don't have no eyes.

Refusing to fight doesn't mean you're a coward

Although most cowards do live long.

It's best to walk away

It might keep prison from being your home.

Not saying don't try to protect yourself

But take a different option if you may.

Don't let your temper rule your mind

Most time it's best to walk away.

Audrey M. Virges

A soft answer turneth away wrath: but grievous words
stir up anger.

Prov. 15.1

DON'T BE TOO COMPLACENT

Don't be too complacent

For a change will surely come

Believe it or not eight times out of ten?

It won't be a comfortable one.

Don't take situations for granted

Nor the people in your life

Not mom, dad, sister or brother

Neither friend's husband or wife.

Don't be so attached to things or people

That if separated from you; you wouldn't want to live

For they are only lended to us for a while

To love, to share, and to give

Don't be too complacent, for in one minute

Your life can change

Then you'll have to re-adjust, recuperate and rearrange.

Keep your guard up at all times,

And too complacent don't you be.

We don't know what changes life has for us.

To that door we don't have a key.

CHILD BEHAVIOR

Children act out different behaviors

As they learn and grow along.

They have to be taught clearly

That bad behavior is wrong.

As you nurture them and teach them

Sometimes putting them in times out,

Discipline they don't care for

Most times they'll cry and pout.

Parents and caregivers don't get discouraged

When their behavior don't change overnight.

Keep loving and working with them

Soon their behavior will change to right.

Audrey M. Virges

Children, obey your parents in the Lord: for this is right.

Eph. 6.1

LOOK YOUR BEST

God made us beautiful

And that's how He wants us to look.

We should be well groomed

Like the pictures in a catalogue book.

We should style our hair and trim our nails

And iron our clothes so neat

And look presentable at all times

From our head to our feet.

Your clothes look nice when they're matched

As well as the shoes you wear.

It doesn't mean that you think you're it

It just means that you care.

Being well groomed is an asset to you

It's not about a contest,

It's about caring about yourself

And looking your very best.

FORGIVE

Forgive the one who did you wrong

For they'll only keep you down

If they're ever in your presence

You will very quickly frown.

Don't give them the pleasure

Of keeping you all uptight

Go ahead and forgive them

And make everything alright.

If you don't forgive the pain is on you

In a most disturbing way

That person you won't forgive?

Is going about really enjoying their day.

So get a grip and humble yourself

Make it the way it's supposed to be.

Go ahead and forgive

And then you'll be free.

Jesus saith unto him, I say not unto thee, Until seven times: but, Until seventy times seven.

Matt. 18.22

ENCOURAGING WORDS TO THE CHURCH

Psalms 121:1-2 says I will lift up mine eyes unto the hills, from whence cometh my help.

My help cometh from the LORD, which made heaven and earth.

Just a few words of encouragements from me to you

When we are encouraged we are inspired,

And more work for the Lord do we want to do.

I know you say this sound like a poem

That seems to have a rhyme,

But it's the way God gave me my encouraging words

To you that I can more easily hold them in my mind. I would like to encourage

The church as a whole,

But first I'll break it up into parts,

And I'll start first by saying to all our choirs,

Keep on singing from your heart.

I would like to encourage our Directors, our musicians, Bro. Lawrence, Bro. Ricardo, myself and Bro. Craig, keep on playing God's music.

For none of us do you have to beg.

I would like to say to the praise team

Keep singing from your heart.

It's your voice that kicks off service on Sunday

Morning, O what a wonderful and joyful start.

I would like to encourage the Deacons,

Keep doing your job so well.

It's wonderful how you give aid to the Pastor

And by his side you dwell.

I would like to encourage the ushers,

Keep lending a helping hand.

Whether it's getting the Pastor a glass of water,

Or simply handing someone a fan.

I would like to say to the Superintendant and

Teachers, keep coming out opening up Sunday School and
to the Church

Keep attending class

Learning and remembering and applying the golden rule,

Our Secretary keep recording those minutes,

Come on in the sunshine, come on in the rain.

For that job has got to be you calling cause

Not one time about it have I heard you complain.

I would like to encourage our missionaries

Our mothers, fathers, youth, boys, girls, men, and women.
Come on to our

Missionary meetings.

It pleases God when we come together and discuss his

Word as to each other we greet.

We would like to encourage the kitchen committee,

The decorating committee, and the cleaning committee as
well.

You're doing a wonderful job. O! Can't you tell?

I would like to encourage Pastor Orr, and Rev. Virges,

Keeping preaching God's word. Keep preaching .

We know the task is not easy, but just you preach on.

For God give you your sermons to help pull someone out

Of the pit, that heaven will one day be their home.

May I encourage the church as a whole, keep lifting Jesus
name each and every day of our lives.

Life is not easy.

Trials will come. Trials will come we're not exempt.

We're not exempt from the trials of this life, yet laughter
will always be.

For it takes both actions to make this body live, one mind
carry them both you see.

So let's encourage ourselves, and let's encourage each other

That we can make it through no matter what the task.

God is truly able if only him you ask.

For one of these days when this life is over, we want to hear

God say "well done my true and faithful Servant.

You fought a good fight, you kept the faith, you finished
your course,

Come on up a little higher.

May God bless you. May God keep you.

ABOUT THE AUTHOR

I,Audrey Virges was born in Chickasaw county, Mississippi, on December 31st 1959. I graduated from Houston High school after which I attended Jackson State University. I am married to Mr. Samuel Virges of woodland, Mississippi. We have three children Craig (Tracey) , Samantha, and Jeremy Virges. We have two grandchildren Craig Jr. And Jaylon Evans. I am a musician and Sunday school teacher at the New Prospect Missionary Baptist church, Woodland, Mississippi. I am a substitute teacher as well as a recruiter and educational director of the regional Global Network inc. I am an entrepreneur. My life is full and I am very blessed.

This book is dedicated to the Sherrod and Robinson Family.

Audrey M. Virges

Contact Page

Audreyvirges @yahoo.com

www.audreyvirges.webs.com